POEMS: SELECTED AND NEW

I

Light through Leaves

Selected Poems: 1968-2012

II

Between the Worlds

Selected Poems: 2012-2016

III

The Intimate Journey Divine

2017

Mary Zettelman Greer

Copyright © 2017 Mary Zettelman Greer
All rights reserved.
ISBN: 1979471878
ISBN-13: 978-1979471879

Table of Contents

Introduction   7

Light through Leaves (1968-2012)

I. First Poems (1968-1980)

Morning	13
Let Us Not Forget	14
Strike Away Doubt	16
Until There Comes a Destination	16
Old Song	17
Naming the Children	18
Letter to My Daughters	20
A Good Wife	21
Living Alone	22
Growing Old	23
Loving the Good Man	24
If I Leave This Land	25
Lifting Up, Touching Down	27
Inheritance	29
Yielded	30
So Much More	30
For My Daughter Driving Away	31

II. This Truth with Emptiness (1980-1995)

The Way It Is	35
Home	36
What Freedom	36
Names	37
A Community of Flight	39
We Have More to Learn	40
Driving Homeward into Danville	41
For Those Who Sit in the Shadow of Death (Luke 1:79)	43

We May Seek That Fairer Country	44
One Moment, Christmas Eve	45
Keeping the Watch for the World	46
Echo Hill	48
Early Red Rising	49
Everything Gone Before Becomes Luminous	50
Keep My Next Step Faithful *(Hymn 277)*	51
Hold Fast	53

III. Morning Where I Stand (1995-2005)

Quietly Here	57
Waiting Here with Loss	58
From Another Realm	59
On That Night	60
We Must Make Ourselves Ready	62
What I Hope Most for the Children	63
Where You Will Find Me Now	64
Psaltery	66
Loving the Long Grass on Echo Hill	68
Passing the Autumnal Equinox	69
They Show the Way	71
Winter Visit Far from Home	73
Preparing to Sell the House	74
Under Snow Content	76
Those Forty Years	77
Gift from Her Deathbed	78

IV. Claiming the Shining Now (2005-2010)

Redeemed for the Journey	81
The Cartographer's Skill	82
The God Visits Ohio	83
Be Reassured	84
From Where I Live in This Earth Town	85
At the Bedside	86
The Structure of Leaves	87
Fall Raspberries	88

Remind Yourself That You Are Never Lost	89
At the Window on a Snowy Day	90
Divining from Shore: The Nature of Faith	92
Something Makes Ready	93
Everything Here Came from Afar	95
His Homework (For Maj Ragain)	96
Looking West	97

V. To Bow and Bend (2010-2012)

I Look Up	101
Into the Harvest	101
Listen to This	102
There Is the Way	103
In the Wilderness, the Solitary Place	105
He Opens the Way	106
What the Midwives Want to Know	107
Urgent Plea	109
Make Bread	110
I Ask This of Myself	111
Pruning the Orchard	112
Beginning Again	113
This Is the Lesson	114
My Little Plea	114

Between the Worlds (2012-2016)

Route Ten, El Paso	117
Out of Night	118
Grief Endures	119
We Are Not	120
Gratitude for All This	121
Everything Remembers the Rose That Blooms in the Desert	122
Let Us Consider Our Way	123
Kitchen Poem	123
The Lesson	124
Even the Chairs Know	125
Three Reflections	126

One Hot Day	127
The Debate on Waking	128
There Will Be One Last Day	129
The Sisters	130
The Sun	131
I Suppose	131
For the Moment	132
Some Day, You Will—	133
What I Saw in Winter	134
Work in Our Little Orchard	135
Written on the Scroll	136
Welcome the Dead	137
Alarming News from the World Again	138
On Your Graduation	139
Little Prayer	140
Asked Again and Again	141
Your Next Step	142
Thinking Always of Endings	143
The Creek at the Foot of the Hill	144

The Intimate Journey Divine (2017)

After the Ice	147
The Intimate Journey Divine	149
Into the New Year	151
When You Are Ill	153
Despite All We Have Done	155
Love Poem	157
After More Bad News from the Arctic	159
Another Spring	161
Winter Melt	163
Lamentation for the Wounded	165
Although the Redwing Blackbird Has Already Returned	168
A Good Day to Hay	170
August in Ohio	172
Here Is Truth	174
The Call to Work	176

Introduction

The three collections of poems in this book loosely follow the chronology of my life. The first of the three, *Light Through Leaves*, presents selections from 1968 to 2012, the difficult years as I wrote, raised four children, taught high school English, and woke. The second, *Between the Worlds (2012-2016)*, contains selected poems written after the children grew up, I remarried, and I found a teacher. The last collection, *The Intimate Journey Divine (2017)*, reflects my sense of the mystery ahead, like an open pasture gate, a faint track leading over an unknown hill.

I admit to the educated reader of poetry that the first 37 years of my writing were entirely without audience, constructive criticism, or study of the craft. It was not until 2005 that I met Maj Ragain, whose great gift of seeing and calling forth the voice in his students at Kent State University opened a door that I had not known existed. He taught us to read and read, to write and write—and showed us how to follow the path to the lodestone buried under scree, as he does in his own work.

In the last five years, I have worked as an environmental activist concerned about the impacts of the fossil fuel and chemical industries on our forested, green Ohio and our planet. What I learned has contributed to my sense of urgency; the recent poems come from my fear that time is running out.

Time does in fact run out. I feel keenly how we travel on the bridge of mortality to our real end, for geologic time in its thousand ages continues to catch us all under the drift. There is no turning back, only the going forward. This is the journey divine, and I long to have rightly honored this elaborate community of soul, cell, soil, and water when my little step no longer touches down.

Acknowledgements and Thanks

Heartfelt thanks must go to my grandfather, Arne Oldberg, for showing us his faithful, daily practice as a composer. I can find no right words here to express my love and thanks to the following, all of whom brought water when I had no water: my parents and sisters; my children and husband; Maj Ragain—who said, "Yes, come in!"; and so many others, friends and Friends. A final thanks to Ellnetta Larson, who proved to me daily that "There is a way, a holy way" by the life she lived in our home, from 1943 to 1956. Hers was the gift of a lifetime.

Light through Leaves

Selected Poems: 1968-2014

I	First Poems	(1968-1980)	p.11
II	This Truce with Emptiness	(1980-1995)	p.33
III	Morning Where I Stand	(1995-2005)	p.55
IV	Claiming the Shining Now	(2005-2010)	p.79
V	To Bow and Bend	(2010-2012)	p.99

Section I: First Poems

(1968-1980)

Morning

From the kitchen door
I watch the morning mist
lean into grassy banks.

A crow is sudden,
sleek in flight
and black,
chill dawn bleak
against his night
of feathers.

Called out of sleep,
rich with prayer
and dreams,

still as this grey dawn,
careful as slow time,
I begin again,

frail, uncertain,
stepping
into day.

Let Us Not Forget

Full summer,
morning.

The August haze pales the sun
standing in the little bowl of land
beside the creek,
a wheat-gold sphere of space
against dark woods.

Heat settles.

Locusts call,
fill the hillside
with bright metal tones,
chants rising opening
falling narrowing again
to stillness waiting,
then rising
calling once again.

Here where earth hesitates,
where light hovers,
I stand between the past
and time's pattern
spreading out
like children in a field;

they come back
grown, smiling;
how strong their arms,
their striding
out upon the land;

and in the pause,
there is in August
a heat and locust day
when I am taken
by how summers
come again,
rise slowly
in the turns,
ascending

through the fullness
of leaves
to the heat-white sky,
and all the sisters
in the fields
are memories
told
to strangers.

Strike Away Doubt

Come outside
and smell the night.

The rain new in air
drives up damp dust,
the food and waters
of the rich-soaked earth.

The spring night wind
demands us,
leaves us tasting,
starving for
its secret nutrition.

Until There Comes A Destination

White empty light,
the sky is low
with winter afternoon
and fine-screened rain.

Dark trees hold silver drops,
strung delicate above
the old, flat, day-stale
snow below.

My heart
like afternoon
is empty;
I move slow
in learning
I have nowhere else
to go.

Old Song

Here's how we sang it
when we were young
and our hearts beat
when the music began:

O love is fine,
and love is handsome,
gay as a jewel
when first it is new;

but then we took poison,
we drank up our portion,
all the years pass.

Something wanders the streets,
stands on the threshold,
comes in at the door
for you left it open;

it searches, touches
the secret places
you almost remember—

downstairs
runs the daughter;
she flies like sparks,
slips through like light,
she gleams, she's gone—

she has taken
the poison
too.

Naming the Children

Like travelers of old—
those walking out
of Egypt—

name your children
for the places
you stopped—

Stranger,
for you were a stranger
there;

Household,
for the pots, the tools,
the unfolding and folding
of clothes,
raising and lowering
of tents,
the hundred ways
your hands worked;

Hope,
for the innocent starts,
cheerful beginnings,
over and over;

Forgotten,
for your eyes were
on something else.

Or—
make baskets
of whatever is handy:
of grasses or thorns;
lay therein the children,
set them into the river
to be given the names
of the gods
of that country—

and pray
they one day
reclaim
whose once
they were.

Letter to My Daughters

Forgive me
that I paused too long
on salty land.

Forgive me
that I drank up the days
in the company of children—
I thought we swam
in our proud green seas
in all those years,
together.

But do you not recall
the grand yellow sun
filling rooms,

the rush of wind
in pines,
the meadow by the creek,
shallow-flooded
after rain,
that shimmering warm pool
spread out upon the grass?

You played there
like river otters,
or like saints walking
on the lovely water—

Do you not remember?

A Good Wife

This is a day
I live
without thought
for myself.

I am generous,
yielding, thoughtful,
and kind.

This day
leaped up
to shout summer
with green leaves,

to shout July,
sun boiling off
car fenders,
children about,
doors banging.

The day bounds
from summer;
spends all—

while I politely
wish for grey fade
of twilight,

wait for the day
or summer
or time
to go by,

still a good wife
though I have
no husband.

Living Alone

I would lie in the sun at the foot of the hill,
I would spread my blanket by the creek,
down where the grasses part and sway,
where the dragonfly glitters at my knee,
and water curls brown to root-bound banks,

except that I have seen snakes there often,
come upon them, sleeping, silent.
Snakes too lie in sun, in warming grass.

If a man lived here,
he would have mown this field
by now.

Growing Old

I

A day, another day,
winter proceeds,
spiral turns of earth
beneath the low white sky.

Night braids the shadows,
brings their midnights
skin to skin.

By day
a pressing on;
by night,
like a fingered narrow ribbon,
a secret slips away to dark,
not quite remembered.

II

Driving home at midnight,
the world's crowned in black
above the clean cold open roads;

small and silent
in the streetlamps,
long canals of light
unfold, allow
this passage through.

Loving the Good Man

The good man's
like a horse:
in his breathing,
a sweetness,
in his eye,
a great mildness;

he is the sea creature, silkie,
asleep warm and sighing
here on the sand
before going back
to the sea,
to deep water;

he is the bear:
ambling and swaying,
making the woods crash
and licking his paws
for honey—
one blow
will kill you.

If I Leave This Land

I will tell you how
  the sky in winter
  spins frozen sweet milk mist
  into the white woods
  where trees stand
  cooling their feet
  in snow,
  holding up
  to the markets
  of the winds
  their woven basketry
  of crowns;

and how
  the fog waits
  hung above
  creek ice;
  water moves through
  packed white banks
  in great slow curves,
  shines like black enamel,
  carves secretly
  the tough and dangerous
  sloping lip of snow;

and how
  the sky,
  a low white shawl,
  is flung out
  by the winter woman
  making up the beds
  of fields—

she settles
  hard white sleep
  upon the hill
  and on the black oaks,
  along the boughs
  of chilled green firs;

and how I am afraid
I will sleep blind
beneath the snow,
then wake in spring
to the sound of melt
running under grass,
find myself
gone—
not knowing,
not remembering
this little hill,
this creek,
this stand of trees,

or that I belong
to that woman
who keeps the shawls
and holds me
in the windy circle
of her arm.

Lifting Up, Touching Down

I have children
but I have
no family.

In my old house
on the hill
I was always
walking lonely
out of life;

I was a veil
of cloudy light
hung above fields
grey, brown;

I was fog
rubbed down
to wet earth
and grass;

or fine snow,
needles
in white air.

All those years
I lifted alone
into dark
like a scent
of earth
in late winter
rain;

at night
touched down,
a wind torn
from the Arctic,
skimming ragged pines
from northern stars.

I was invisible,
or the wind,
or the beseeching
of trees;

I worshipped
under trees,

waited for
the coming
and the flying out
of leaves.

Inheritance

I lie down to sleep
in snow-steeped afternoons,
when the deer too,
down by the frozen creek,
lie down.

In the clearing pines,
in snow,
in ice-stilled air,
white day,
they patiently await—
spring, perhaps sun—
or night.

Their endurance feeds;
their dwelling
and their silence
nourish;

they abide—
what can Earth will
to us?
Winter, star, morning?

Lie down quietly,
alert and listening—

we will live
or we will not.

Yielded

Days crest, unfurl,
ride one after the other.

Time, the only now,
is an ocean
like the air,
the light—

and chance within
each rising, falling tide
is promise and enough—

and hope is how
we take the wind,
let currents steer.

So Much More

In afternoon,
wind rinses
summer leaves
like water rushing
over stones;

when wind stills,
leaves stand like water
in dark pools
by banks.

Lowly evening spreads
from shady woods,
sweet with dusk,
damp—

so much to feed on,
enough to live on,
wind and leaves,
water,
night.

For My Daughter Driving Away

I left the lights on
so the house would shine
across the star-dim field
and through the vapor
of the frosted air,

so you,
swung out upon the turnpike,
could turn to see,
to say goodbye,
through night and fences,
tangled waste,
goodbye
to gleaming, gold-flung
home.

You didn't, you tell me.
Your van was windowless.

The road took suddenly
to unknown terrain,
the highway's foreign country,
uncharted and remote
within our very fields.

But we, at home,
we slept till dawn
within our radiant bath
of streaming light,
our bright beacon
of the well-lit house
unassailed by night,

and sent you,
leaving home again alone,
gleams shining
on your hair
and in your eyes,

your journey into night
and dawn,
calling forth the light.

Section II: This Truce with Emptiness

(1980-1995)

The Way It Is

From these back steps
where I sit chilled,
the air smells sweet,
of coffee, horses,
distant water,
wet earth,
winter grass.

The dogs and I
must raise our noses,
turn our heads
to pull the scents,
to sort, to name
them.

In my half-century,
time has warmed,
cooled, warmed,
like this spring sun,
veiled by grey cloud,
then unveiled.

The clarity of dawn
distills a perfect light
above the scaffolding
of trees,
this truce
with emptiness.

Home

Late afternoon grows cold,
old, stoops down to dark.
The windows spring up
black and fierce.

Downstairs a single lamp
cups its small space
against the shadows,
against the still rooms.

What Freedom

I came home
late tonight,
walked under stars,
the great white moon.

I crossed the white grass
under still trees
to windows yellow-filled,
lamplight from within
as quiet as the waiting
after prayer.

What freedom
to come home alone.

Names

I sit in the open door;
rain has rinsed the air.

The green grass
streams summer;
the dogs and I
assemble here
on the edge of morning
to consider names.

I do not want
a father's name,
an old man's name,
a young man's name.

Is my name
clouds that coast sky,
edges faring out
to seek the free air?

Is my name
black
as pine tree trunk
against the light,
a dark door
standing open?
I can slip through
narrowly
to some bright
other side.

Is this name
sorrow
or gold flecks
in a dog's brown eye?

My name is nearby now—

in the tree perhaps
where leaves
dip and sway,
rain tapping down
through their green faces,
to shower the air—

or it is scents
on summer wind
traced by
dogs' ardent noses,

lifted and working
the threaded currents.

A Community of Flight

Saturday,
the morning drained and still,
doors open to the melting snow,

we pause, we listen,
rise happy to the wing-drum
of your wild goose coming
before we know we hear
your heart-sweet voices.

Nearing, clamoring,
you break the sky,
take the roof,
and drive on
cloudward,

and at our window pane
we ride your wild calling;
we follow as we pierce
wind, space,
thin, cold air,

then
return to rooms,
to little day,

while you beat on
beyond the woods.

We Have More to Learn

Look upon the details
of old dogs.

In the morning,
sitting by them
on your back door steps,
study them,
their honesty
of gaze and whiskers.

They watch the woods,
the creek,
raise their heads
to filaments of messages
on the rise and fall
of wind,
read the whereabouts
of things
and distances.

They breathe in lightly,
shape the invisible,
prove the life
you do not even
guess.

These are the beasts,
lying like lions in prides,
casting long looks
across domains,
measuring sound
with separate ears,
swiveling alert.

Sit quietly beside
their serious shoulders.

They teach willingness.
They show the way
to be discreet.

Driving Homeward into Danville

The great slow plain
of Illinois
reaches east and west
for miles
to states not my home state,
to foreign-seeming lands,
Ohio and beyond,

to the eastern coastlands,
or to mountains
at the distant rim
of western highlands.

I can breathe
out here
in these fall cornfields,
on the roomy floor
of all the world,

beneath the high grey sky,
the strong, broad
Midwestern sky.

Years ago
when I came home
to Illinois,
I watched for God
to come again—
the radio
said he would—

on a staircase lowered
from silver clouds,
bands of light
streaming in flat rivers
to the humble prairie.

Along State Route Twenty-four,
land pushes to the sky
like sea,
black-turned
furrowed fields roll
and unroll outward
from the wake of highway;

chopped tough
cornstalk stems
foam to the edge
of white horizon,

breakers tossed up
shredded gold
on the dark soil face
of the land's expanse,
the solid fundament
of the world.

Late afternoon:
sun gleams
on low round crests
of plow-cut soil;
evening hangs rooms
in yellow cottonwood groves,
pools in shallows
in the grass,
ponds of light.

Here I am again
under this same sky,
on this wide land,
sailing these rich fields,

the farthest distances
the signs
of my redemption,

all my life a leaving
and returning,
navigating
by the center line,

hope
an old hymn
on the cornbelt
airwaves.

For Those Who Sit In the Shadow of Death
(Luke 1:79)

Day holds to grey,
a skim milk shadow
underneath the broad white
cloud screen reached
across the sky,
a continent of leached
and ashy light.

My kind of day.

No sun calls,
no wind routs.

This is death,
the warrior pilot
pale as web;
he casts his veil
around our shoulders
in this drained time;

he takes our causes
into empty streets,
he is heavy as
late sleep—

his terrible design,
to ride beside us
coaxing from us
a crossing
into mist,

promising
his white art
as we fade.

We May Seek That Fairer Country

We thirsted
and the great drought
pulled green
from new sweet
water-scented grass;

we thirsted;
summer stooped,
a dry old man.

No rain for days
since first shoots showed
at the rising arc
of summer's heat;
now hot wind
rushes the hides
of leaves
like fire spreading.

This parch of heat
robbed the garden,
choked us with chaff,
burned cancers
on our arms.

While we dreamed
of rain,
there was no rain.

Perhaps we rise now,
walk away from
the straw and yellow
earth;

perhaps we take
our old gods
with us.

One Moment, Christmas Eve

In winter
when the woods fall
still and white,
we leave the spirits
to the brittle cold.

They live
among the trees;
the woods are starry
with their eyes—
soft snow sweeps
to us
their voices
nearly heard.

When I walk
the woods,
I am well-known,
I know.

Indoors,
we forget them,
then pause
to bend the knee
to the godliness
of the pine-sharp tree,

its lights,
signals
by which we call
our greeting
to those ancient ones
outside
in icy night—

then having blessed,
and being blessed,
we once again
forget.

Keeping the Watch for the World

May morning.

Old women waken,
choose to live,
or pray,
or prepare
for this day's work.

A black crow squalls
once from the pine;
his shadow skates
the green-gold hill.

From the west,
in spring-thick fields
across the road,
the steady crashing
of great metal echoes
to the eastern rim
of woods—
cutting roads—
   forty luxury lots,
   for sale,
the sign says.

Bulldozers grind
beyond the call
of mourning doves.

Old women
do not fear
machines
that come today
to tear the skin
from grassy fields,

to eat the little thickets
where deer sleep,
to crush the bones
of trees.

They might forget
they carried out of sleep
the chill of having waked again
without their own consent—

yet morning steeps;
they sip its grassy-scented
healing tea.

Old women
lift their faces
a few moments
to the sun,

watch fiercely
from their open doors
when little girls
are playing
near the men
who drive
the tractors.

Echo Hill

Old house:
graceful ship
that sails the hill
westward toward
the distant fringe
of trees—

you breast
the yellow fields,
you pause here
in the tide of light;

your one hundred-fifty
years of voyaging,
has held
the children
in copper sunsets,
clabbered skies,

in all the shining nights
black as wells,
dipped from the universe
around.

Early Red Rising

Grey morning light,
a quiet out-of-doors.

On the fine thin
icy edge of spring,
the silver sky
drives snowbeads
misting on the hill,
sheering on sharp-angled
currents of the wind.

From the open door
the cold white air
springs sweet,
ice-water strong.

From the woods
beside the creek,
red is rising,
the early red
of stems and branches,
gathering, clouding
in the brush
and rising—

the dogs,
let out,
run down the hill;

when I call—

they don't
come back.

Everything Gone Before Becomes Luminous

After the storm,
in late afternoon
we drive to town.

The stony sky
moves east
before us;

a ledge of darkness
leans wide
above the washed
black road.

Behind—
where evening sun
springs clear,

the road shines
fine silver
between green
and fragrant
grassy banks;

in the rearview mirror,
we see
where we have been—

traveling a river
of flashing light.

Keep My Next Step Faithful
(Hymn 277)

It seems
I am always traveling
to a home
I have never known,
walked the stony banks,
called on God,
but still
I have had
so much fear.

I'm sitting it out
in this clean light
on this winter day.

Sorrow is gold
worked to fine foil
and laid over
our failings.

Last night
the moon
white as linen
lay its cold light
between us,
showing us
how we breathe
alone.

From the rooftops,
last snow stippled
the coils of wind.

Spring will sing up soon
from the muddy lowland,
from the pine needle lap
of the woods—

but the old yoke
wakes upon me
each dawn,

its dark wing covers,
its bitter corm
feeds the rootstalk
of fear.

We who doubt
float far
from the faithful
and innocent trees,
from the good soil,
the strong stone.

We do not understand
that everything rises,
everything always
is sailing away.

Hold Fast

Become a tree.
Know heart-wood.

Let root take
in dark soil,
let hands learn
work.

Look up
as leaves lift
to heaven.

Break, do bend,
be taken down
or felled or fired—
but like the tree,
you will not travel.

The secret growing
center holds.

Section III: Morning Where I Stand

(1995-2005)

Quietly Here

A little space
is quiet
in the rain.

Green mist
stands down
among trees,
black secret shadows
under firs'
sloped wings—

always in Ohio,
rain.

It taps and stipples
boughs
where leaves
are poised
as if for flight;

rain drinks air
from a milky cup,
the watery breath
of woods, of fields.

We move quietly
in the gentle household
of the rain.

Waiting Here with Loss

This morning
men are cutting down
a tree across the road.

When their saw stops,
I hear their voices.

On this March morning,
winter litter lies
strung and scattered;
the snows have swept
the leaves and sticks
of months
against the steps,
against the house.

The hill is silent—
not spring yet.

What bird calls,
saying: listen, listen—
its solemn whistle
from the scrubby woods
cries again and again.

The tree across the road
drops cracking limb by limb;
sundered branches,
splintered architecture
of the crown
crash upon the berm.

We are broken branchwood;
we wait for March fields
to lie back, to open,
to tremble
into fine pearl light.

From Another Realm

We saw a snake
on a desert road.
He lay long and straight,
a ruled design,
bright glossy black
and gleaming white,
elegant as the king's own law,
precise and technical,
a royal snake.

He gathered suddenly
in coils and power,
he swam the yellow gravel bank,
stroked swiftly
at a rock rise,
left us like slipped folds of silk,
or mythic water in a dream
that winds itself upstream.

I longed to know him.

On That Night

I came home last night
and found you gone,
doors wide open,
windows lit as bright
as yellow candles;

I stood outside
and called into the dark—
Where are you?
and you called back,

Down here—

The hill lay down
within the fog,
the sharp wet grass
clean and black.

I followed
hillside stepping stones,
breathing
pine-cloud darkness
to the stand
of hemlocks
at the round hill's
ancient edge.

We are down here,
you said;

I found you
sitting
on the tumbled wall
of barnstones,
talking
with some friends.

Nice night,
we said.

The moon was
something silver
mistward, eastward;
the leaves gave up
night's nutrients
of smells,

the fog
a strong infusion
of the night and moon,
steeped in vapors.

Well, I said,
*I know now
where you are—
I was wondering.*

And looking up
from the slow black creek
and bank of pines,
the house above
stood out to sky
like some great schooner
unmoored
off the coast
of childhood—

your voices
dropped behind
in misty dark
as I walked toward
the distant lights

considering
when to sell
the house.

We Must Make Ourselves Ready

The song of the cicadas
swims into morning,
rises above the canopies
of leaves
and falls away again;

the trees stand up
into the mild milk sky;

leaves of trees whicker
and run, washed
in the little breeze.

Summer gathers herself
to walk away
across the field.

What I Hope Most for the Children

The mild moon—
white coin of light—
rides into the blue-milk
sky.

From our front step,
a cloud range piles peaks,
an unmapped land.

And now that you are gone,
my little ones,
my little tribe,
I hope for this—

that you find
golden air,
live companionably
alone,
taste how sweet
each evening.

Where You Will Find Me Now

We live
in a stream
of light,
in the wash
and charge
of time.

Here am I
on this same hill,
for twenty years,

and again
autumn shines,
the day as clear
as shallows
of a lake—

clear
as shallows
where
as little girls
half a century ago
we swam safe
in warm water
over yellow sand—

where
we raised our eyes
beyond the serious deep
to the far rim,

the dark line
of distant pines
edging the banks
like knives.

Now, this day,
a leaf skims
to the steps
at my feet,
a corn-yellow fiber
wind-brushed
from a tree woman's shawl,

the shawl
she wove and wore
in the summer
of her intricate dance.

Let me remember—
to look to trees
to teach me time
and the generations
of trees—

how they feed
on light
in sunny mornings
on this hill,

where
for this day,
I stand.

Psaltery

Indian summer—
the wind calls down
through oak trees' leaves,
washes their tops
at the woods'
swarming edge,

spills broad, abundant,
sails the high crests,
returns from far
to the warm bright yard
with a god's voice
in the stirred hearts
of the great trees'
crowns.

Wind rushes down
from blue sky
into slow yellow
day—

a cheerful, strapping
wind that sways
the lonely willow,
weaves maple limbs,
trembles among young families
of round and friendly aspens.

Silver-flashed
tossing leaves
sign to the sky—
the wings of the woods
rustle and stretch—

and light
stands clear as
lake water,
flickers down

to pools
of black shadows
laced in the gold
and the green grass—

telling
the holiest
secrets.

Loving the Long Grass on Echo Hill

Beloved hill,
after cold fall night,
strong rising stems
of unmown grasses
reach and stand.

They are tough-fibered
thin green ribbons,
economical of life;
they own the earth.

They breathe
their patient sweet
and green
into yellow morning air.

Every blade of grass
wears dew,
left behind last night,
the smallest of stars
caught shining
on sharp,
clean edges.

The grasses sway
and run in silver
when the wind
curves low;

they bend and gentle,
willing to lie under us
with right humility—

and when we die,
they bring us back
to light and night,

bring us
to their anonymity
in the humble pasture
of the earth.

Passing the Autumnal Equinox

The rain is silver,
the sky, the wind
fast and shining—
and the edges of the clouds
gleam like sterling.

The trees tremble
their little yellow leaves;
blooms of leaves
shear off
into the golden woods;

swarms and schools
of leaves uprise
over amber shoals
of light,
flocks of leaves swarm
like a shifting flight
of blackbirds
swelling over fields
of fall.

Blackbirds lift
from crowns
of yellow trees
above the road;
they pour
into the slatey sky
above our driving;

the flocks flood out,
shirr in, a fleet
of overpouring,
rushing all away,
bright black stars
flung up to ride
the white and rainy air—

and sweeping out,
our own dear Earth
swings round
to dark aphelion,
yellow leaves
in her wild hair,
all flying.

They Show the Way

Pines
have taken
all the land;
it is their winter.

They stand
serious and dark
above the remnants
of windy fall.

The pines stand
by the road's edge,
dark,
they are crows,
they are night.

They hold
secret shadows
underneath their spread
and layered wings.

They raise
their planed black sails,
stretch into windy white
with perfect reaching.

Beneath their sloped boughs
in the cones and tatters
of their rusty needle-pillowed
footstools,
there is no shelter
with these winter lords;
the bone-bare cold
sharpens still and clean—
no message left
below;

and upward
from the sinewed lap
of roots,
they arrow
to the sky.

Against the overcast
of clouds,
the round limbs grow,
one by one,
spokes
of measured step,

telling how
pine grows,
how learns
to reach and peak,

Learn how
pine holds
life safe
in the desolation
of the cold.

Winter Visit Far from Home

We traveled
this winter
to Florida,
the way people do.

How would
I live
in Florida?

I would become
a tough black crow,
fly into salty wind
above the rags
of foam;

leap on wings
over green stone
seawater waves,
threaded veins
of white;

I would cry power,
victory, rage,
robbery;
I would scavenge
chilled sand beaches,

I would snatch up life
the wind has pestered
from the humbled
who walk
the gritty sidewalks,

leaving them
far below
to wear their thin coats
and grow old.

Preparing to Sell the House

Clean out
the rooms
for strangers.

These rooms
will feed them
on the pale
winter light
lifted white
as new paper.

In the stillness
of chairs and tables,
the family of things
patiently wait.

This is the hill
where the children
foraged
the knife edge

of north winds
that rose
against the windows
all winter.

From this door,
tracked snow
marked the paths
of their going,

torn snow
like whitecaps
on the swells
of a winter sea.

Now the white drift
presses through
to crushed grass,
to the hidden hill,

its dark soil,
reverent with history,
spring
not much farther
below.

Under Snow Content

The broad sky
opens to white.
Earth hums
in secret,
under snow content,
already in possession
of the hidden.

I, my small self,
wash and fold
blankets,
stack wood,
count candles,
test the sharpness
of our blades.

Meanwhile—
all around—
the work of winter
stills and deepens,
draws drifts
over the placid soil,
soothes the meek grass
of the swales.

We, the housebound,
step carefully
in the snow-hushed
places,
upon the white,
upon the thriving
unseen.

Those Forty Years

What did the wanderers,
home-going seekers,
long desert walkers,
believe in
all those years?

Choked on manna,
croaking with thirst,
no water-sweet mist
rising from Nile marshes
just before sunrise,
nor steam
from new-turned soil—

no courtyards lovely
with women's voices,
no stooping to tend
the dear, the orderly
hearth!

Didn't the children
learn to love
each bleak horizon
new each morning,
and one day would they too
think it good to roam?

Their youths, their maidens
played in the narrow way
between campfire light
and wilderness dark;
their dreams
were foreign dreams.

What did the tribesmen
hope for?
What bloom of the desert
slaked?
What end of the world
did they await?

Gift from Her Death Bed
(For Ellnetta Larson)

We prayed we too
would one day say
our glad goodbyes—

like the scholar
who saw how sun
streamed through
the stone arch
warming
the holy word;

like the woman
washing vegetables—
she looked up
from her pan
of cool water,
grateful;

like children
who lay
in tall grass
behind the house;
drowsy with summer,
they waited to be called
for supper;

like the midnight swimmer
rolling over to float
on his back
in the black water
of the lake—
under stars,
over stars,
drifting—

like these,
for a moment,
not afraid to say
our glad goodbyes.

Section IV: Claiming the Shining Now

(2005-2010)

Redeemed for the Journey

A life is no longer
than the length
of this wood table
set for food,
dishes among tools,
letters, prayer,
loneliness.

These are the known:
landings, hallways,
steps, stairs,
back door paths,
light glancing
from this window,
that open door—
all the ways of home—

but the grassy slope
behind the house
leads upward,
crests,
thins into countries
of high clouds

where fields are wind,
the river, the rushing air—
and the destination
to the horizon,
a blue surround—

all flaming up
and claiming
the shining now.

The Cartographer's Skill

I thought that
when
I moved to town,
the spirit woman
of the summer
would walk
the green and empty hill
back home—
that she would call me
again and again,
and hearing no reply,
cease calling—

I thought that
when I drove past
my old house
I would see
just some remnant
from her last year's skirt
blowing in the field.

However,
she has found me here
among these little houses
that comfort one another
like children resting
close together
on the grass.

Perhaps
she rode here
on the wind—
or my liege the oak
called her,
told her
my new address—

for she has known me
long—and keeps
the moving map
of constellations
and my journeying
on the palms
of her hands.

The God Visits Ohio

Summer is full now,
strong,
has settled himself
here in fields
flooded in heat
and yellow sun.

By the roadside,
the sweet green
of high grass rises
from his shoulders,
a fragrant steam.

He sleeps
under broad and glossy
leaves of oaks,
dark in the shady
cool of crowns;

he hums his dreaming
from the swale
of cattails
down by the lake,
from black water
standing in
the grassy bog.

He wakes to ride
the flying cloud heaps,
brushing out
white vapor scarves,
calling drowsy distant
thunder down the sky—

he never notices that
we are all in love
with him.

Be Reassured

Here
there is always
plenty of grass.

It is always under the foot
or swelling to distances
on the rising and falling
of fields,
sea swells of land
rocking us ever
to sleep
and to life.

The charitable grass
is green, giving,
faithful to the eye,
merciful to air.

It strokes the world,
lavishes its work
on the wind
and unfolds lowly,
humble and cheerful
even to the edge
of the woods,

coming to the courts
of the noble trees.

From Where I Live in This Earth Town

When white fierce stars
above the summer oaks'
black crowns
shine through,

I think the women
of the distant sky town
bend to the fabric
of their quilting.

I lie down in grass
upon my back
beneath their frame
to watch the prick
of their light needles
stitching star shine
in their midnight
making.

Like old starlight,
I am so many years
behind,
slow as seeds
to stitch down
fitted pieces,
to draw through
threads,

slow to bind the layers
to the whole design
on this plain backing
that we below
lie down
to see.

At the Bedside

Dying child,
little fish
in this ocean
sweet and salt,
bitter, bright,
rushing full
to God,

you swim here
gold and quick
among us
in our shallows;

you venture
near the banks
of human lands.

We call,
you brush
our little nets,
the lures we cast
upon the light-struck
deep;

you dart away
and rest
beyond us;

left behind,
we pray you find
the streaming tides,
the coastal current,
all that great sea—
we cannot
follow.

The Structure of Leaves

Leaves:
they are houses
of light,
where elements
of earth
look through
green shadows
into sun;

leaves are
the milk of earth,
feeding air,
tasting the yellow pools;

they are food,
sweet with simple sugars,
herbs brown and dry,
or bitter as rue,

and fibrous,
cutting, deadly—
be careful
of leaves as food.

See
how the leaves are
capable, clean,
always knowing
what they are,
what to do.

Leaves are work—
like praises and requiems
of singers,
like words
the prophets send forth.

Read in the language
of their veins
what will come
to you.

Fall Raspberries

By whose intricate design
do these detach so gently
from the stout integrity
of their seeds?

How be so tender, fragile, sweet,
as red as blood within the vein,
so much more faceted than my words,
so much more useful than my honoring?

You have brought the ancient message
of a great nutrition
to this appointed moment.

And you return through light
to earth with sure submission.
I would live my life so too.

Remind Yourself That You Are Never Lost

Find your way—
in the winter,
even new snow deep over fields
is not entirely without tracks;

yeast
in the bread you knead
always will seethe upward
from the bowl;

a word that whipped
when you were small and thin,
a dear point on your compass
now.

Find your way—
white fog that hides the footpath
is a fine sieve holding clouds
of sweetest water,
to your face, your hair,
your unknown thirst.

At the Window on a Snowy Day

A siege of sun
fills the windows;
I wear
a coat of sun,
am held
in the broad hands
of the sun.

Outside the windows,
days' snows
are drifted deep,
white snows
unfolded and fallen
in plateaus like linen,
new-ironed flatwork—
easy as sleep—

as death.

From my window
well I remember
the gentle deceit
of snowfields
in sunlight—
they deliver
shining praise,
leaped-up light
and glitter
off gold-flecked
swells—

how these snowfields
call us to them,

*Come out,
walk here!*

For we are like dreamers
who choose to walk
to the lying-down place
where the psalmist
promises—
none can keep alive
his own soul.

Divining From Shore: The Nature of Faith
(Remembering G. M. Hopkins)

Tonight
upon the frozen lake
I saw three men walk
the ice field slow,

one before, testing,
one behind, the follower,

and from the bobbing
ever farther from the shore,
the last,
carrying a light.

Beyond the milky mist,
unseasonable
and white,

it was odd
to see men walking there,
where most times,
only deep black water
shines;

undoing, strange,
to see men moving
upright so far out from land
upon a lake,

slowly
disappearing low
into the darkening night,

and wonderment,
to see
their clear light
rising, falling
with each step,
to distant shore,

and never
out of sight.

Something Makes Ready

I drive home Route Forty-three,
late winter, late afternoon,
in falling water-heavy snow.

The pines wear white
like sheets pulled up
around their shoulders,
like tall young men
sitting up in bed
at night alone,

watching fields
reflect the broad
white paper light
of snow.

Little low grey lakes
I pass are smooth
as paving stones,
steel ice pools, opaque,

beneath them hidden,
the coarse and tangled
life of plants.

Under snow-melt,
reeds' and grasses' stems
rise twining
to the thawing silver water
as slow as memory
of the time
before the ice came,
so seeming long ago—last fall.

The car's wheels mill
a slurry of grey run-off,
a bitter, salty soup rushes
to culverts
at the distant edges
of the town,

and beyond
the frozen thatchwork
of the fields,

the black creeks
trickle, seeking
the white roots
in cold soil

thirsting for
first water.

Everything Here Came from Afar

In the field at night,
I walk out with the dogs.

They move silent
over wet leaves;
they pause,
fierce, taut,
listening.

Obediently
I too lean
into that black wing.

Behind,
yellow lights
of home
recall the dear,
the comfortable—

out here,
we search night,
raise our noses,
taste grand winds,
broad outpouring sky,

lift our heads
to catch the first rain
spun from a salt
and southern sea
a thousand miles
away.

His Homework
(For Maj Ragain)

Write
to praise
the way
light falls
and flashes
on the leaves
on summer mornings—
June mornings,
rather,
this morning
only.

Gold stands
like washed glass,
clear in the air.

Every leaf shines
like silver,
like stars,
like the glistering
wind-wrinkled
water.

Blades of grass
stir in yellow floods
of sun in this lake
of light—
here,
you make your strokes.

See the shimmered rivulets
part and fall, streaming
from your hair, your arms
and shoulders,
as candled in the blue of sky—
you crest and rise,
breaking the surface.

Looking West

Enfolded in twilight,
this is the time of the day
I return to again and again.

Copper foil
of last light
follows the sun
down the west,
draws away,
over the blackening rim
of Earth.

This is a finite time.
We turn to the circles
of our small yellow lamps,
friendly and poor,
coaxing us back;

we wait in the falling light
for the great shadow
of a whole world.

Then, darkness:

fields of night in the sky
stretch down to the waters,
to the lowest lands.
Even the stubborn grass
lies invisible, cloaked
in dusk.

Day done,
we are there.
Now we lean
to our work
in the unseen way—

the journey begun
after dark.

Section V: To Bow and Bend

(2010-2012)

I Look Up

Into the courts
of the morning mist
a deer comes
down to the lake
to drink,
bows
to the shallows.

May the water
be sweet,
may your thirst
be a reasonable
prayer.

Into the Harvest

We are up to our eyes
in the vegetable garden;

every step bruises leaves,
their green smell so thick
we are nourished
and fainting
at the same time.

The dishpan overflows
with bounty;

who can see
beyond this moment?

Listen to This

You must change your life,
the poet said.

One day in high summer,
the leaves will rattle in wind,
the sun flame yellow,
the locust song rise and fall.

The very earth itself
will lean from today,
carry our bones
and our wealth
into the mouth of winter.

This will change
how we should call you,
how you will know yourself,
and at what new destination
messages may find you.

There Is the Way

Last night
I walked the dogs
into the dark,
into warm air
after rain.

Beyond the little slope
rising eastward
from the house,

the black curve
of gentle hill
seemed to
fall away—
to be invisible
in white mist
gathering itself
from earth,
from water—

seemed
to cloak
the very end
of earth—

and black trees
far away
to mark the rim
of some other world.

I almost feared
to walk beyond
the crest of hill
and into that seeming void,
lest endless falling
be this midnight
truth—

but I know well
this slope,
this dark—
I know the way
to rise, to trust
a least suggestion
of a dawn,
of light.

In the Wilderness, the Solitary Place
(Isaiah 35:1)

I want to know what secret thing
moves in these woods at night.
I want to read it on the air,

memorize its outline with the senses,
smell its wild cold fur,
seek from its ear, its nose, its tooth,
how sweet it is, how rank,
how of soil, of leaves,
of carrion,
of blood.

Under those black firs,
it crouches, summons all itself,
rises, cherishes sign of me—

I long to learn how to name,
to know its danger.

He Opens the Way

After midnight,
I walk out.

At first,
I see only grass, mud,
close night,
its small alarms,
its heavy arm
curved round the house,
darkening the fields,
the trees.

Then upon the eastern rim,
Orion springs well-armed,
vaulting forests
to swagger sky,
blade, boots,
white fists glittering.

Down here,
on frozen swale,
the brown loam shines
beneath the matted grass,
every leaf now edged
with crackling frost
from distant stars;

the warrior leaps
Earth rolling,
binding us
in his flung light.

What the Midwives Want to Know

In early morning,
first frost stiffens
the thick green grass.

Leaves in the garden
hang low and rigid,
surprised, wounded
by this strange ice.

Across the road,
the gas well men survey
beyond the little copse
of cottonwoods.

One wears orange, to warn,
another carries papers,
wears a hard hat.

Then the sun springs up,
false and warm;
a bitter tea of dew
lies on old wet leaves.

I wonder,
does frost-melt
rise into the tailings
of the thin mists
shifting from the lake?

Or does it sink
to comforting cold sod
and into rich grit
of minerals,
storehouses,
hidden aquifers—

and who comes now
to a beloved field
to sell the ancient secrets?

What careless easy sleep
held us till we woke
to see the giant
bending low and greedy
above the stubbled corn,
teeth among last leaves?

And how if that sweet water
never rose again
through green stems,
a sap for fruits,
the psalm of the mild horse,
bowed to the filled trough,
drinking?

How if thoughtless men
should touch the lip
of every cup
with their exotic poison?

Will we send our children
into fields at first frost
that they might sip,
that we might beg
they live?

Urgent Plea

Children,
hold yourselves
no less dear
than the black willow tree
holds the blind white root
that heaves stone
to seek hidden waters;

or than your own old cat
holds dear
the closing of eyes
in sun,
the drawing to stillness
in the long grass
to await the kill;

or than the hawk
holds the lift under wings
and the open field
below;

or than the tasseling corn
holds honeyed pollen
in the drift
of its blessings—

time enough,
children,
to lie down
among the bones
of the fallen trees,
yours among theirs.

Make Bread

Starter first,
flour and water.

When the quickened cells
begin to breathe,
you will see

the pocking of the gases
of the stars
there in the bowl
you hold
in your own hand—

your very soul designed
for fainting with delight
at its piercing sweetness.

Add and blend
a just measure
of your flour,
the same
the world has always
called for,
one grandmother
at a time,
since before men
made bricks.

Let the heels of hands,
which know already
this old work,
knead the springing dough.

Rest it for a time—
the grain will know—

the second pressing
of the whole
is needful.

Wait, bake,
be patient for time
and the work of fire;
you will be fed.

I Ask This of Myself

When I am old,
will I remember
stars sharp
above dark fields?

Will I
lie down
in long grass
with prayers
of contrition
for broken stems,
or hold the roots
to feed on earth's scent,

snuff air
as bears do,
when wood smoke stings
on winter nights?

Will I cherish the dough
that springs, rises,
ready for the oven,
the steam ascending
from the hot loaf
as a soul rises,
a sure, thin thread?

Will I go down
to the little woods,
to the wet leaves
where felled trees lie
in sour soil,
in that tangle
not lovely,
a coarse little woods
doing its workman's
work—

bringing all
back round
to fullness?

Pruning the Orchard

Speak
when you cross
the drifted fields,
your blades honed,
smelling of sweet oil;

explain
to the apple trees,
humble servants
of the kingdom,
in winter cut back
to willing arms,
all their gentle parts
dropped to the snow,

tell how the shining saw
finds tender pith;
how the pruning shears
take every hope
of sky.

Talk
as you work
of spring,
of how these wounds
bring full the fruit;

teach them
to expect this.

Beginning Again

Let me not fear
on that day
when my soul
remembers,
gathers wholly,
rises fine,

as steam
escapes
the cup—

as morning mist
above the field
thins
in early sun—

as first leaf shoots
part the seed,
uncurl to day—

as the heart wall
vanishes
when someone
opens the door
and says
come in.

This Is the Lesson

Leaves of trees
have stayed until their end,
despite the late fall storms
in these last nights.

I too stay,

seeking
how to hold,
to bow and bend,

having hope
to draw the soul
full through—

and then—

My Little Plea

Don't be misled
by my verses here,
of household, dishes,
garden fences,
my account
of sweeping rooms
or smoothing
covers on the beds—

I am trying to tell you
where God is
in my house—
there: sun flickering
on the morning floor,
or there:
beside those shoes,
still muddy,
by the back door.

Between the Worlds

(2012-2016)

Route Ten, El Paso

Driving westward
on the border:
the comfortable
on our side,
the humbly passive
on the other.

We looked to them—

small dwellings hidden
under distant trees,
little fires burning low
on dry and yellow
mesquite land.

Plumes of white smoke
spread west to east,
a low sweet-smelling haze
of burning husks, raked rubble,
oil in fry pans, horses.

What thing-making
business of their lives,
what coming, going
in each clean-swept yard,

we in our fast car
could not know—

so raised our faces
to our open windows
to sip the leafy smell
of wood smoke,
reminded some people
will survive.

Out of Night

Out of night
suddenly
the coyote cries,
nearer than
our orchard trees.

His wild call,
pack-longing,
seeking, suffering,
uncoils, tracks
over land,
wounds,
is wounded.

We mark his flight
by his unearthly voicing—
where now?
near? Or far?

So fleet is he,
beyond the slope of hill,
through
pitchy night,
into far fields.

The neighbor man
steps from his porch light
into strips of mist
threaded in the pines,
rifle eased
to shoulder,
forestock fitted to palm
of ready hand.

We turn homeward,
hearts pierced
and beating,
wishing that wild
lonesome traveler
well.

Grief Endures

In December,
a strange mild spell.

Water stands
in stiff marsh grass,
sky lowers
in the short light
of winter.

Grief is the shepherd
all through
these quick little days
of his making.

He carries
each one of us
on his shoulder;
he labors
over fields indifferent
under melting snow.

We Are Not

We are not trees.
Trees bow and bend.
They shimmer
in wind.

Change plays
through them.

In cool grit, deep horizons,
their intricate feet search
the truth of water.

They drink light,
feast on air,
patiently lift limbs
despite the storm.

We are not trees.

Gratitude for All This
(Luke 6:38)

This good measure
pressed down
running over

rises fiercely,
like a hurt;
makes the eyes burn
with tears;
its fullness
cannot be compressed.

To the west,
the green trees
have come
to the table
of the morning sun.

To the east,
wind shimmers
in leaves;
their patterns play
over each other
as a run of creek water
strokes its stones.

There is not enough time
in the moment
or in the year
to tell this good story.

It is all too much
for one person
or one story.

Everything Remembers the Rose That Blooms in the Desert

Sister,
we've grown old.

We forget now
those distant nights,
the lean, too-long
afternoons,

such toil
that our hands
fell from work.

We forget that
even our sons
have become old men,
playing and foolish,

that branches
crack in dry winds
that snatch away
the walls of the house—

yet in the last light,
do you see?

All things
stream upward

and we
where we stand
will fill again
and again.

Let Us Consider Our Way

Let us swim
as the beaver swims
toward the shore
of the evening lake:

a little rush
among black ripples,
then a pause,
then a rush—
a peaceable progress—

then his strong dive
to the wattle and willows,
long gathered,
of shelter
and home.

Kitchen Poem

July,
after dinner,
wind off the lake.

I work
in the kitchen.

This soap is sweet,
the water warm—
hands home
and comforted
in the dishpan.

We slip through
as birds in evening
slip the gold light
hung in summer air
to the other side—

where—
as the psalmist said—
night shines
as day.

The Lesson

The dogs gather
in the living room.

One sits watchful
at the window,
surveys the snow,
scans the field.

The other curls
at the foot
of the ottoman,
tucked in round,
close, patient.

They do not need
to wait for death
or to hear
the voice
of great Jehovah;

they do not pause
for the moment
of beseeching prayer;

They are already
obedient, mindful,
ready to arise
and follow.

Even the Chairs Know

Chairs
in the living room
are seated humbly
all around,
as in Meeting.

They are silent
in this morning
winter light.

They do not beg
for any particular
thing.

Arms comfortably
at their sides,
their wood and cloth
at rest,

each one holds
its own good place.

Three Reflections

I

In the coming heat,
high summer day,
the morning opens,
green flourishes.

No one notices
the clock.

II

When I am alone with God,
as in this morning hour,

moments warm and round,
full to the edge,

nothing more can fit—
yet more pours in.

III

I woke, asked,
What will it be
this day?

There will be soup for lunch.

The dog looks up
with wise eyes.

A man told me
his father died;
then for sorrow
he could
not speak.

Three times redeemed
and still early.

One Hot Day

There is nothing to want.
We have more than enough
of everything.

Even the cut fresh fruit
is too varied and colorful.

The green grass is
over-lush,

the trees have rushed
to great green plumes
of overabounding fullness,

their riches of leaves
seethe in the humid air.

The earth soaks—
a warm bath
of July replete,
everything yellow
and green.

The Debate on Waking

Redemption is too heavy
to draw from sleep.

Silence stands in our house
each morning;
I don't wait long—

Awaken, be up!
I hear.

But these old feet
don't even want
to carry me out
to the garden.

Each day rises,
as on a current;

each night slips
into fierce shadow
where the crouched beast
stares—

I am besieged,
I am carried
by moments
hauled one at a time
from a grievous well.

There Will Be One Last Day

It may be a long, quiet afternoon,
sky plain and grey.

One will lie down,
pull up the beloved covers
to feel the close years,

one will see the room's
old friends.

There, an edge
of light,
a pattern in the woodwork
above the door.
Clothes are folded
on the shelf.

This, the architecture of now;
we grip each dear thing anew—
not ready—

the softening current gathers
into shadows—
nearer, that dark gate.

Pause then,
dream a field,
a safe path
from the old house,
that place in the sun
where the wild fox kits
leaped and played—

there,
it will be acceptable:
the yielded breath.

The Sisters

They call
to each other
across rooms,
across countries.

Make me whole,
they cry.

*Once
on the sunny steps,
by the back door,
we were one!*

*In the shade
of the big fir,
I was you.*

Too soon
the green ash tree
floats brown leaves
on winds
from the far north.

One
is going to have to
bring the other
home.

The Sun

When night is here,
the sun is loved
in far countries fair,
sweetening them
in its warm honey;

And here,
when there is no sun,
the lean and darkening sky
is terrible, hungering
with news of wars
and winter.

I Suppose

If the night wind
over new-cut grass
and through fall woods
were food,

we would all
grow thin
and green.

We would not
make war.

Everyone
would be able
to sing.

For the Moment

There is no war here.

Our young men
do not run stooping
behind walls.

Our young boys do not wait
with plastic buckets
at the spigots
for their turn.

Our children
do not kneel
in dirt
writing
with their fingers
as Jesus did,
nor do they ask,
who is blameless—

No—
here we see only
the sun strike
into the leafless woods,
how it weaves shadows
on the unmarked
snow.

Some Day, You Will—

praise God,
loving the mystery
awaiting
your unclothed soul;

praise the day,
the clean cutting cold,
white in sky
and land,
white as the sheets
of winter's slopes;

praise
black tree tangles,
the swale that parts
fields,
the lake bank sloped
steeply down to silver
water.

You will glory
in the fine-sieved
gray light of
the purple dawn,

its chill
draped across
your shoulders
as you stand
at the window.

What I Saw in Winter

I saw
sun sparking
on the newly sculpted snow,
broad expanses
molded like low loaves
of new bread
laid side by side—

and look! A coyote
crosses the frozen lake.
Tail down, head low,
his old coyote way.

He's no grandstander—
it's just the shortest way
between two shores.

Lithe and wild
he is.
Everyone here fears
more of his kind
coming,
for there is nothing
of milk or mercy
in him.

He reaches the bank;
delicately springs
black and ingenious
into the trees.

I want to call him,
feed him, see to him;

but he is not deceived;
he would have
none of me.

Work in Our Little Orchard

These apple trees
are beyond me now.

They are not
the kindly courteous trees
of childhood.

Despite our armaments—
strongest steel,
heaviest blades,
sharpest saws,

these trees,
limbs large and round
as strong men's arms,
these stand against us.

They are grown old,
intricate scaffolding
and leader shoots,
long whips seeking
into pines on
either side,
verticals
like fence palings
impenetrable—
all drive skyward.

Scarce is there purchase
for an edge to thin.

Here in January,
tough bones
of their green passion bare
demand their own inheritance,
leaving us behind
as orphans.

Written on the Scroll

No one can change
the design
of the outer room,
this courtyard
of the Lord.

We are given
utensils:
fine gold, pure silver,
tin, wood, steel, clay,
fibrous plants.

And at the end
we will rise
from our beds
with neither clothes
nor craft—

lift the brocade
at the edge
of the door

and with empty hands
pass through,
leaving
our
meagerly portion
behind.

Welcome the Dead
(For Jim, for Teddy)

Welcome the dead—
they quicken
in the motes
of this day's sun
through bare trees;

they shift
in the lively air,
the swaying patterns
of mothers and sons,
the neighbor's lost child,
your old dog.

Our ancients
and descendants
dazzle the eyes,

gather round our feet,
make anew the map
of the unknown continent
upon the floor.

Alarming News from the World Again

This is not the spring
we looked for.

The wind forewarns
the land,
the lake water
has turned purple
under dark skies.

In the city,
we hear
of youth and death
on the street
where our grandfather
built the house;
in the ocean
currents slow,
warmed like thin soup.

The night air
smells of rain
and the trees bud:

they do not know
what we know,
or they know
something else.

On Your Graduation
(For Samuel Lasko)

Here you see the path,
how it passes
before our little houses.

Some of us, bereaved,
watch from sunny rooms;
others raise their heads
as horses do,
then return
to the close business
of grass.

We don't say goodbye—
after all,
you're not crossing
the Bering Strait!

Your feet know;
you rightly trust
to them.

Nevertheless,
we mothers
and our mothers
from the ages
know another truth.

What we hope
for you leaves
our pastures poor,
on this,
your glad day.

Little Prayer

Let the day
be the prayer.

Enlarge
our clearings,
lest fire take
our homes;

Let us pray
green—
let us pray
water—

Keep us close.

Asked Again and Again

How
in the gold infusion
of morning
and summer

can one waken
incurably bruised,
wounded
in this dark hollow
of heart---

how,
on such a swift,
deft earth,
flung to swing out
in a radiant ocean
of light?

Your Next Step

Faithless children,
birth
did not waken you.

We planted the wheat
and you gather thorns.

Now you are hungry.

You say
it's hard to believe
something unseen
can emerge
from outside
everything real—
after all,
it's a known universe,
yes?

There is nothing here,
in your kitchen,
your tool room
when you glance up—

no something present
in the dark
that presses
before you shut
your eyes
at night.

Surely, you say,
the sky can't be
like the ceiling
of the Sistine Chapel.

Thinking Always of Endings

Tonight our old dog
drags his back right foot.
He trembles, lowers himself
to rest, stops when
pain catches;
he sinks, falls back,
scrambling.

Thinking always of endings,
I am reminded
of the exiles marched to Babylon,
of Jonah's searing despair
when he woke
to the facts—

I think of the men and women,
die Juden, those who left
their violins behind,
who dared not send
their children to school
on that day—

I think of their long winter coats,
fur hats, their coming down
from the freight car
on that country siding.

Who can understand this
when the spring grass
is so green,
when birdsong clamors
from the woods?

The Creek at the Foot of the Hill

Where water was,
there was the map,
the boundary
of the nation.

Its presence led,
saved life,
cooled ashes,
made broth.

Water
crafts the homeland—
here water stands,
helpful, peaceable;
there it rises
and takes the bridge,
the shed, the life.

It rushes out
hot and salty
with the new child's
birth.

Water tells us,

Ride like sparkling
over deeps,
seek the farthest
place!

tells us—

Learn to float!

Water,
you lie under deserts,
you return after drought;

you were once our pride.

The Intimate Journey Divine

(2017)

After the Ice

See:
How the water
continues to rise
in the fields,
under the roads—

seeps,
delivered from the nearby kame,
that meek slope of grass
with its secretive ice,

from low ridges, little eskers
of stony earth,
their cores,
gripped in black frost.

These are the glaciers
of old,
given in sops, in soaks
to the grassy roots
over decades
of kindness—

these are the trickling creeks
unseen under thatch—
for the farmer,
in spring,
his tractor sinks low
in the favored valley
of furrows,
loam over peat;

waters arcane
to the township trustee
in the orange truck—
he knows only cold patch
for the heaved road
after winter.

Walk on the berm
by the reeds.
Note how the way
was marked by the ice,
how it scoured the land,
raked, scarring all things,

how it returns
through its gravel and silt
over centuries,
refining the gift,
washing the wounds.

The Intimate Journey Divine

Is this the home-going road,
this sloping curve
off the highway,
down past the fields
banked by bare woods?

The heart grieves
for this last pass
over low rises,
one after the other,

left by the glaciers'
slow press,
their steadfast advance,
their eked retreat
grinding the land
for thousands
of lifetimes.

We love the worn ways.

When we go out
to walk,
the dogs gather round,
then tack off
across the hillside,
heeling back
with glances
of intelligent
regard.

We wade
the shoals of grass
as the dogs veer and return,
range and retrace,
mapping the land
with their youth.

We are taking
the intimate journey
divine.

Our steps are discrete,
they are numbered.

Count the ways
to leave this self,
this plaited mass,
the afflictions
of land, air, water,
first minerals
dissolving in our bones.

Perhaps
this is the winter
we shall thin
like mist
over the lake—

no more need
for our coats,
our boots left behind
by the back door—

this, the winter
we rise,
stroking the folds
and the fields
with devotion.

Into the New Year

This year
we will kneel
at the side
of the marital bed
to tuck up the sheets
and the blankets
of forgiveness;

we will kneel
to greet the old dog
waiting alone
at the end of the hall.

In the kitchen,
we will kneel
by the table—

look for
that little broken thing
that rolled off
to the floor—

look,
until it is found.

Let us kneel beside
the white bathtub,
guard the children—
like seals in the water,
they sled
the shining slopes,

we will kneel
with our gathering towels
to these little boys
and girls
as they shiver
into our arms.

In spring,
we look
to the morning
when we kneel
in the crust
of late snow,
for the merciful green leaf
will appear;

at night,
we will kneel
under the framework
of stars
where Earth hangs
in their lattice,

saying
O Earth!
for this most tender
of homes.

When You Are Ill

My dear,
we can't fear
that dark thing,

its shadow
moving over
the white sheets.

Our hands lie
beside us
on the covers
as if asleep;
now thick,
they can
no longer
mend the torn,

for the needle
is too fine to hold,
the eye too small
to thread.

See how
the crows rise
from the last corn
in the stubble,
how the hawk
leans
against the wind
above the field.

So many
we must leave
to their urgent
errands!

This is our eventide,
abode of the weary,
the worn—
we are gleaned

as an oldest star
draws back
its light—

to what?
a flaming out
like praise

or the open pasture gate,
the green grass
sloping away
sweet and fair.

We are engrafted
at the last,
dozing
into earth,
to rich loams
where the tree
reaches down
to gather its riches
together.

Despite All We Have Done

Something of the old,
first good remains
in fields.

Our feet know this.

It rests patient
under new grass
where snowmelt
crackles
through white roots;

it slopes
with grace
the curve of swale,
broadly palmed
by twelve thousand years
of passing ice.

Something wild
breathes here still,
from the time
before we knelt
to mark the corners
of a dwelling
or cut the loam
with our sharp tines
of steel.

Food steeps here:
leaf bits, silt,
fine rock—
these fold
in their dark meal
the reaching seed
that longs to thrive
and finger
toward cool water
far below—

seed that wants
to open
its whole self
like wings.

Now,
this spring,
this great heave
of soil,
worked by rain,
soaked to sponge,
rises
to new bright
day.

This field—
ours,
(we like to say,)
tilts its face
to sun—
humbly spreads
before us,

willing so
to feed,
to let us rest
against its shoulder
while we live,

and later
to hold dear
our dead,
cradled
in the green.

Love Poem

I want to learn
to be kind—

as the green
gathers
under the brown skin
of trees' limbs,

as thick flood water
after days of rain
sluices in ditches,
pours through culverts,
rinses the sands
and clays
for the fields—

kind,
as when spring comes
snow melts into soggy banks,
holds the cropped
and tender roots
to the lip of earth
so they may
drink their fill.

I want the kindness
of rich loam,
sifted from the bones
of earth
in the new garden,
how it opens
into the hand—

I want to be kind,

for the sun returns
after the wind settles,
and easy day pauses
at the back door;

always kind,
for you come patiently
with me to the window
to see the lake,

how the wind draws
sleek water over water
in silky folds
of silver and brown.

After More Bad News from the Arctic

This is the news:

Old water seeps
from the dark ice;

it is clean, holy, first.

My soul—
this little fish thrown
to the creek's sloped bank,
lies half-dazed with gasping—

urgently needs
your living melt.

Or pasture me,
I pray,
in some grassy field,
its sweet steam rising
in warm sun;

I have known
your sighing breath
of old,
the hour I was
newly born.

And You,
who feed the worlds
from your hand,
who dip into realms
of richest provision—

I too,
for my few timid steps,
this my short day
soon over,
my tentative crossing—
need the fine ground meal
of your bread!

I am too late,
too late and longing—

though
the wind sweeps
the silk of the lake
as your hand
smooths sorrows,
mysterious beloved One.

Another Spring

What shall it be,
when I am too old
to see the lake?

Already,
in this slow rain
I cannot see
to the trees
on the other side,
and fear
I have never—
despite the decades—
known them.

Heavy drops
bead limbs,
hold themselves
dense and gleaming
in the watery air,

refuse to fall—
although
before the end,
they must.

The maple trees,
grey rain infused,
draw earthen broth
to their million flowers.

Look how male and female,
pendant together,
pale green,
dipping and spreading,

demand, compel the fruit—

abundance
running over,
the bounty!

The Unseen
powers and presses
crown-ward
to the newly tender,
drives into living sap,

holds within
the wise and aging heartwood,
ring by new ring—

yet
as it is with trees,
the pith
no longer lives;

pith—no use
to coursing flow,
pith—locked within,
imprisoned
at the core—

so it is
with me,
standing at my window,

from First Day
when the forest began,
to this.

Winter Melt

Water,
you are
the elder brother.

You come
centuries
through old rock
and heavy lands
to winter fields.

If we were horses,
we would brush you
tenderly
with our long noses.

If we were dogs,
we would taste
your ancient
mineral seep.

We,
in our places,
are new,
young!

Our day's light
comes and goes
around us
as birds
swoop and retreat
in the sky.

Nothing
on our side
of Earth holds
your ministering wisdom,
has traveled
such far horizons
below the seen.

Nothing on our side
teaches us the comfort
of darkness
or gives us
such promise
of the deep.

Lamentation for the Wounded

Little grove of trees
in that low place
near the cornfield,
I come to you.

You host the world.

Your children,
seen, unseen,
trundle
chore to chore:

beetles, ants,
dragonflies, daphnia,
earthworms,
a million micropeople;

even ferns' spores
in leaf layers
leave their fronds,

minds set steadfast
on first life's light,
then a pinch
of supper.

You open weir and way
to all your daughters,
teeming sons of daughters;

then bowing low
you tuck your cells
under litterfall and duff
to sleep
into the dark.

I, I come
panting, blundering
like the big black dog
escaping from the neighbors—
he ramps through your homesteads,
plundering your crops,
your courtyards;

we both smell wrong—
I, of medicine,
the dog, of meat.

We are unclean.
We have no roots,
no mouths
scrubbed in forest loam,
rinsed in leafy rain.

I kneel here
at this hospice bedside
of your people.

In your villages,
your huddled
tree roots,
seeping hollows,

you count losses
from the strands
of protein
of your ancient
weaving—

you know the number
of your dead.

We have wounded
your dear ones
with our indifference,
our chemicals and our greed.

So fair were
your beloved children
succoured in the soil,
eating soil, making soil;

you made our kingdom
as we ravished yours.

We never even
learned your map
of cherished gardens,
your tender
once-savored
world.

Although the Redwing Blackbird Has Already Returned

Each morning
I do not know
where to begin.

There is war
somewhere;
I look over the trees,
I expect incoming
as wild geese
to the lake.

I tidy the cans
in the pantry
for the next generations
to find.

When I hear
of a chemical spill,
the wounds
of Earth burning
cry in my ears.

Grief bruises
the heart,
like the young airmen
who wear
their new jackets
with pride
before they take off.

Mourning scathes
the spirit,
like the black youths
who smoulder
in ashes,
terrible and knowing
the unjust world.

We shall creep
on our knees
to the floor
by the bedside;

there we shall say,

trust not
in horses,
airplanes, kings,
prophets,
men who come
after the storms,
your children's teachers.

There we shall say,

Help me,
my Lord, my God,
turn the stiff wheel,
this ponderous ship
of old bones,
away from the shallows.

When spring comes,
light pours clear
into the trees;
they satisfy their thirst
with water
loved by loam.

And what of us,
who wait
at the window?

Stand at the bottom
of the cloudless day;
cast thought
toward heaven,

though a bird
flying over the reeds
be silent,
bringing you
no help.

A Good Day to Hay

My daughter's husband
goes out to cut hay.

This is our window,
he says.

Enough of green.
Not gone
to brown seed—
not wet
nor too dry.

He waits
for right weather.

A little wind
sweeps the high grass—
the fields bow and bend,
lowly and graceful,
as lake water rolls
in swells
to rounded banks.

The rich harvest
rushes up
from the land.

West of here,
above the broad steppe
of continent,
a great storm gathers.

Orange fury
of Earth and death
simmered in heat
boil up
from the cornfields
of the Illinois till plains,
relentless
in black wind shear
and rain.

But
this is our day.
We bathe here
in golden light—

as the tall grasses
fall to the blade,
lie flat
on the warm field,
swath by swath,
life over life.

August in Ohio

I

Now turns
Earth again.

Mist steeped
above the lake
at dawn
rose here
or over the far Pacific—
or Babylon's valley—
a million years ago.

Every water drop
has washed the continents
again and yet again,
rinsed all the air,
sweetened untold forests' leaves,

passed as blood—
clear or gold or red
through every wing vein,
carapace and claw,
and your thin wrist.

II

How foolish
are we,
mowing, sweeping,
making,
to think the day
is ours—

we are as corn
that first uncurls
to light
from dark fields;

so soon it flourishes,
heavy with gold sugar,
strong with shining leaves
like broadswords,

then each stalk
must bow
to the blade.

So in our season,
flung
to the high blue
August sky,

we shall kneel
to the harvest,
to the will of earth—
shall enter in.

Here Is Truth

I continue to believe
the day is mine—
these vegetables,
cut for broth,
belong to me.

This is my day.
I am the child
loving my toy dishes,
my doll's house.

You
who are Lord,
King, Friend,
the Father,
the Maker and Holder,
you fill this,
my little room—

You
press beyond
my painted walls
to flood the fields,
the distant trees,
the great Earth,
your floor.

You broaden, rise,
swarm the sky,
you hold fast
the moon
and beyond the moon—

every flaming out
and bursting atom,
roaring wind.

Even in black lonely death
by drowning,
capture, crushing,
or sleeping—

there
you stream,
full, love-ramped,
pouring the oils
heavy with comfort.

You
knead and smooth the soul,
this intractable Man,
fusing the seam
to the guiding flange;

You
compel the marrow
that seethes in the ply,
exacting the alloy,

You,
O tender victor.

The Call to Work
(For Your Birthday: James William Greer)

We,
so armed, so hungry;
so intent
upon our footsteps,
we are insatiable.

We are little colored beads
that ornament the fringes
of the millennia
in the childish patterns
of our tribes and homelands,
our humanity.

The years are horizons,
one over another
till the soil is rich.

God opens His hand,
the seed falls
into the fruitful field.

Waste not one hour
of your portion
of His sowing
and the harvest—

all this
will be turned under
again and again.

CPSIA information can be obtained
at www.ICGtesting.com
Printed in the USA
LVHW032345020821
694324LV00004B/872